THE TOWN'S STORY
by Michael Senior

ACKNOWLEDGEMENTS

The photographs on the following pages are by courtesy of
The Author:
4, 14(A & C), 18, 20(B), 22(B), 28(B), 30(C,D)
E. Emrys Jones:
2, 8, 10, 14(B), 16, 20(A), 22(A), 28(A), 30(A,B)
Cambridge University:
6(A), 6(B)
National Monuments of Wales:
6(C)

ISBN: 0-86381-345-3
Printed and published in Wales by
Gwasg Carreg Gwalch,
12 Iard yr Orsaf,
Llanrwst,
Gwynedd,
Wales.
☎ *(01492) 642031*
Fax: (01492) 641502

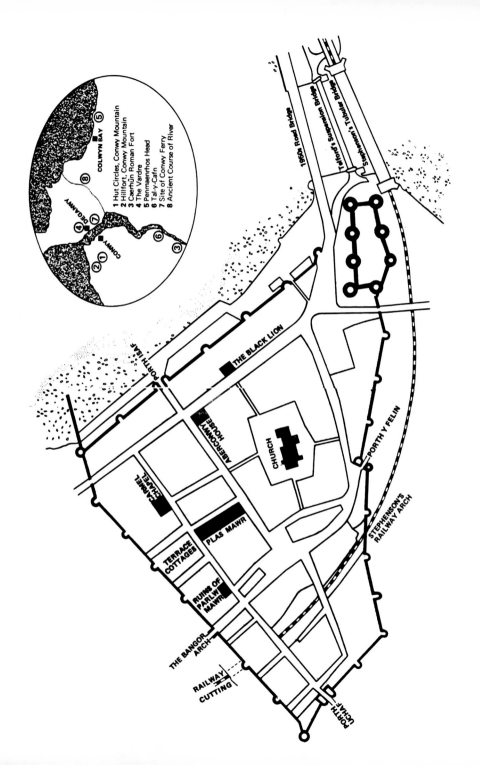

COLWYN BAY

1 Hut Circles, Conwy Mountain
2 Hillfort, Conwy Mountain
3 Caerhûn Roman Fort
4 The Vardre
5 Penmaenrhos Head
6 Tal-y-Cafn
7 Site of Conwy Ferry
8 Ancient Course of River

DEGANWY

CONWY

1950s Road Bridge

Telford's Suspension Bridge

Stephenson's Tubular Bridge

THE BLACK LION

PORTHISAF

ABERCONWY HOUSE

CHURCH

CHAPEL

PLAS MAWR

TERRACE COTTAGES

RUINS OF PARLWR MAWR

PORTH Y FELIN

STEPHENSON'S RAILWAY ARCH

THE BANGOR ARCH

RAILWAY CUTTING

PORTH UCHAF

Preface to the Revised Edition

W HEN I wrote *Conwy, The Town's Story*, in 1977, I thought that was it. History, after all, should not change. Since then several great changes have overcome Conwy, of which, in 1977, we were totally unaware. It had not then been decided how to solve the traffic problem.

The tunnel is the most obvious of the changes that have occurred in Conwy since then. I deal in some detail in my book *The Crossing of the Conwy* with the historical background to the decision and with the construction process itself. Here we shall only mention these, and pay more attention to the immediate results of the tunnel's construction and of the by-passing of the town.

One of the results of the by-pass has been a change in appearance of the town (and consequently some of the photographs used in this revised edition are new). Some of the town's main areas are now paved and redesigned. Much restoration has taken place, both of ordinary dwellings and of the town's great buildings: Aberconwy House, Plas Mawr, and Telford's bridge. There is a new entry to the town through Porth y Felin, and the town walls have their wall-walk open for almost the complete length.

Nevertheless what is still striking is that amid a constant pattern of surface change the underlying personality of Conwy remains the same. A town's character is such a vulnerable thing that one might have expected it to have been effectively destroyed by now. Conwy's secret is that it is a lived-in town, and its surface texture is underpinned by a strong sense of community. You can tinker with its superficial appearance, but it seems that you cannot, thank goodness, change that.

Michael Senior,
Glan Conwy.
January 1995

When you look around yourself in a place like Conwy, the surroundings which you see are inevitably the outcome of a long and complicated process. The intention of this booklet is to consider how the past has given rise to this present in which we live.

Beginnings

A NY explanation of Conwy must really start with the river. It was because of the river that the place came into being where it did, and indeed the river has governed much that has happened to it since. It had of course been there for many thousands of years before men started to form settlements, using the line of a rock-fault to drain the upland dome sometime before the ice-ages. It was probably when the north coast became blocked with ice flowing south from Scotland that the river changed its course, from an outflow further east breaking through a ridge of rock between Conwy mountain and Deganwy to reach the sea through what is now Conwy Bay. So for at least some tens of thousands of years it has been flowing past this spot.

There have been people here for much of that time, too, although the earliest stone-age hunters have not left much that we can look at. In prehistoric times the lower land was covered in forest and was virtually uninhabitable, so that when people started to build dwellings and to graze animals, they did so only on the barer ground of the uplands and where the trees grew at a lower level in the salt wind of the coast. That is why the mountain above Conwy, Mynydd y Dref, the 'Town Mountain', still bears the signs of so many very early habitations. (Ordnance Survey map reference SH 760 778.)

The coast of Wales was always vulnerable to invasion by seaborne tribes seeking new territory, either from the south, from continental Europe, or from across the Irish Sea. As their technical ability developed and they became organised into larger units, the people of each area began to build themselves defensive compounds on the tops of hills, often overlooking the sea. During the last few centuries before Christ, these became the hillforts so often recognisable in coastal Wales, of which the one on top of Conwy Mountain is a particularly good example.

These were iron-using people, part of the tribal spread of nations dominant in Europe at that time, people whom we call Celtic because they spoke a Celtic language, the ancestor of the Welsh language which is still spoken here now.

*'Caer Lleion', the pre-Roman Iron Age hillfort
on top of Conwy Mountain.*

5

'Canovium', a Roman fort on the west bank of the river, seen from the air as light-coloured lines in the fields; the present parish church of Caerhun occupies one corner of the site of the fort.

In an aerial view the extent of the castle at Deganwy, on and between the hills of the Vardre, can be clearly seen.

A solitary piece of masonry is almost all that remains of Deganwy castle, demolished by Llywelyn ap Gruffydd in 1263.

We know about them mainly through the eyes of the Romans, who were expanding their empire across Europe at the time when the Celts were building the latest of these defensive forts.

The Roman Empire continued to spread, until it even reached as far as North Wales, and when it did, in the first century AD, it established the importance of the crossing of the River Conwy, a crossing which was to play so much part in the area's later history. The Romans actually crossed some miles upstream at Caerhun, and built there — just as Edward I was later to do down-stream — a large fortified camp to protect the crossing-point. (O.S. SH 777 703.) They understood the importance of rivers for provision of supplies, which no doubt could reach them here round the coast from Chester; and they saw the importance too of the joining at such places of land and sea communications.

The Romans came and left, in the space of about three hundred and fifty years. No doubt the existence of their camp on the Conwy had in the meantime played a part in establishing this as an area of habitation. When the troops had gone the threat of invasion from the sea returned, and what was needed now was a main defensive site from which the rulers of North Wales could control the coastal approaches.

The tribal communities which had built the hill-forts had by the fifth century A.D. become organised into kingdoms. Here in north-west Wales the tribe which the Romans called Venedotiae had founded the kingdom of Gwynedd. It was no doubt because of the fear of invasion from the sea that its early kings established their seat on the hill across the river, the Vardre, where remains of habitations from the early post-Roman period onwards have been found. (O.S. SH 783 795.)

Under one of these kings North Wales became unified and powerful. The legendary character of Maelgwn is associated in early literature with this hilltop in Deganwy, and indeed archaeology confirms that there was a prosperous court there in the sixth century A.D., the time when King Maelgwn lived. It was from this first recognisable Welsh king that the later princes of Wales claimed descent.

From this time on Wales became increasingly a nation in its own right — and increasingly pressed by the neighbouring country which had come into being in the meantime, formed from the amalgamation of the various kingdoms of the Angles and the Saxons. A long period then followed, before the Dark Ages gave way to the Middle Ages, during which, while great events such as the unification of England and the Norman invasion took place elsewhere, the history of Conwy did not progress at all.

The Abbey

*I*N those early times there were some people who came westwards for the sake of peace, for seclusion from the now increasingly active world. The first people to settle at this spot on the western bank of the river were a community of Cistercian monks. It was quiet here then, and they carried on their simple lives undisturbed, fishing and praising God. It seems that the white monks first came to Aberconwy in 1186, and we know that the Abbey which they founded here was of sufficient importance to receive official recognition from the God-fearing ruler of North Wales, Llywelyn ap Iorwerth, known to us as Llywelyn the Great, in 1198. Llywelyn's charter of that date, written in Latin, marks the year of the formal foundation of the Abbey of Aberconwy, and so of the beginning of our town.

> *Be it known .to all the sons of Holy Mother Church, both present and future, that I, Llywelyn son of Gervase, Prince of all North Wales, by the intention of divine piety, for the safety of my soul, and of the souls of all my predecessors and heirs and of my successors, have given and granted, and by this present Charter have confirmed, for me and my heirs and successors, with full and perpetual independent jurisdiction, now and for ever, to God and the Blessed Mary, and to the Monks of Aberconwey, servants of God of a regular order, this very place in which the same Monastery has been founded by these boundaries, as follows. Rising from the Conwy river to Abergyffin, thence along the whole length of the Gyffin river . . .*

But trouble was already looming on the eastern horizons of this blameless community in this lovely spot. Just as the Roman Empire had spread gradually westward until it reached the Conwy, so now the Norman lords who had become, among their many other titles, kings of England, began to look westward for new acquisitions. They could not rule comfortably with independent princes such as Llywelyn so close at hand. A long period of territorial competition between the Prince of North Wales and the Earl of Chester reached a first climax in 1211, when King John brought an army to support the Earl's cause, and marched along the coast as far as Deganwy. (O.S. SH 783 795.)

The west tower of St Mary's parish church in Conwy is based on the remains of the Abbey church, all that is left now of the Cistercian monastery, founded at Conwy in 1180's and removed by Edward I in 1283.

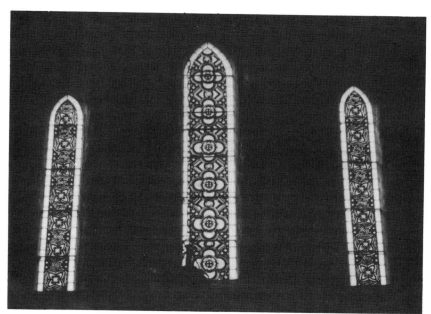

In the west wall, perhaps a part of the original Abbey church, the three fine lancet windows and the Early English doorway remain as a reminder of the simple idealism of the Middle Ages.

Looking down from the site of Deganwy castle one can see the narrow barrier of the river; defended on the western bank by the Welsh, it kept the English from entering the heartland of North Wales during several invasions in the 13th century.

There he came to a halt. The barrier of the river once more came into prominence. The army was virtually besieged on the Vardre, and retreated to the border after suffering a period of near-starvation. King John's son, Henry III, continued the attempt to bring Wales under the control of London, and in 1245 an English army again reached Deganwy. Again the river confronted them at their feet, a small but sufficient obstacle. That September à soldier in the army wrote home to England:

> *There is a small arm of the sea which ebbs and flows under the aforesaid castle (where we are staying) . . . This arm of the sea lies between us and Snowdon, where the Welsh quarter themselves, and is, at high tide, about a crossbow-shot wide.*

Across this small barrier the two forces faced each other, fighting from time to time. When the English dared to cross the river the Abbey of Aberconwy suffered its first shock of contact with the world which it had come here to avoid.

> *Our people then returned . . . and, like greedy and needy men, indulged in plunder, and spread fire and rapine through the country on the other side of the water, and, amongst other profane proceedings, they irreverantly pillaged a convent of the Cistercians, called Aberconway, of all its property, and even of the chalices and books, and burnt the buildings belonging to it.*

That, unfortunately, was a taste of the sort of life in store for Conwy during the next few hundred years. Evidently the Cisterican monks, if they wanted peace, had come to the wrong place.

Edward I

KING Edward I, Edward Plantagenet, nicknamed Longshanks, was the grandson of King John — just as the prince against whom he launched his attack into Wales, Llywelyn ap Gruffydd, was the grandson of King John's enemy, Llywelyn the Great. Edward had visited Deganwy as a prince, in 1256, and no doubt looked across the river then at the land still held by the Welsh. When he became king in 1272 he set about completing the long struggle with his neighbours which he had inherited from his father and grandfather. At first he was successful, and Llywelyn signed a treaty with him, in the Abbey of Aberconwy, by which the Welsh prince would retain the part of his principality west of the Conwy. But the Welsh had never been satisfied with their mountainous heartland alone, and the war over the border country went on.

Something of great importance to the future of the area of Conwy had happened in the meantime. In 1263 Llywelyn finally pulled down the castle at Deganwy, which had been taken and retaken, destroyed and built again, and in the end proved to be too useful to the invading forces. As a result all that is left of it now are a few fragments of walling. When Edward launched his last campaign into Wales he decided not to rebuild a castle at Deganwy, but rather to take the crucial step of crossing the Conwy river. And here, on the Welsh side of the river, he would build the fortress which would protect this vital crossing.

At first Edward made his headquarters further east, at Rhuddlan, where he even called a Parliament, and from where, in the March of 1284, he issued the Statute of Rhuddlan which imposed on Wales the English administrative divisions of shires and boroughs. It was by that Statute that the Borough of Conwy was formed, although by then a start on the building of the castle and walled town had already been made. The status of the town as a free borough was confirmed by a charter in the same year.

Edward, by the grace of God King of England, Lord of Ireland and Duke of Aquitaine, to the Archbishops, Bishops, Abbots, Priors, Earls, Barons, Justiciaries, Sheriffs, Reeves, Ministers, and all his Bailiffs, and his lieges, greeting: Know ye that we will and do grant for us and our

From the air the layout of the walled town shows how it and the castle were built as a single unit of defence, an extension of the idea of a keep surrounded by a bailey, representing the peak of the development of medieval military architecture.
(Inset) Edward I and his queen Eleanor, sculptures in the choir of Lincoln Cathedral.

13

Some of the tops of the battlements were decorated with small pointed stones, called finials, to lighten the appearance of the towers.

Traces of the limewash which originally whitened the castle's walls can still be seen.

An 18th century etching shows the castle jutting out on its rock over the water, an effect now lost due to the building of the bridges.

heirs that our town of Aberconwey shall be henceforth a free borough,
and that our men of the same town shall be free burgesses, and that the
Constable of our Castle of Aberconwey for the time being shall be the
mayor of that borough . . .

Before this grand plan could take place, however, the Abbey, which was right in the middle of what was to become the garrison town, had to be removed. Edward was respectful to the power and influence of the Church, and sought, it appears, the consent of the Pope to resite it, since, as the resulting Papal Bull explained to the unfortunate monks, "your Monastery for many reasonable causes could not remain conveniently in the place where it then was." The whole Abbey was removed to Maenan, eight miles up the river, and resettled there, protected by numerous rights and privileges which the king, by way of compensation, gave to the monks. There it stayed until the Dissolution of the Monasteries. (O.S. SH 789 658.)

There is nothing to see of the old Abbey of Aberconwy now, but a vestige of its physical presence has survived in the older parts of our Parish Church. This was the Abbey church before the removal to Maenan in 1283, and it then became the Parish Church of the new Borough. Some parts of the base of the tower of this present church date from that period, and these are all that we have left of the original settlement at Conwy.

The purpose of the Charter and of the removal of the Abbey was to introduce into this new fortress town a number of English families, to form a colonial outpost to administer Edward's new regime. These, with the official rank of burgesses, were to be tempted there by the granting of rights and privileges and by exemption from taxes. Since he succeeded in enticing into Conwy less than a hundred families, we can guess that these incentives were not enough to compensate for the discomfort of living in an unknown and probably hostile country. Conwy in those early days had plenty of space within the walls.

The castle and the walled town were built as a single unit. What is remarkable about the building of it is that it took only a little over four years to complete, being started in the March of 1283 and largely finished by the autumn of 1287. We can still see signs of the way in which the work was done, the stones being wheeled to the tops of the rising walls up ramps supported on timbers sticking out from the masonry. The post-holes into which these were fitted still spiral up the towers. When the castle was completed it was surfaced with a white limewash, traces of which, after nearly seven hundred years, are still visible. The construction of such a massive building is in itself a notable achievement, but what is even more surprising is that it was made not only functional but beautiful. Such details as the finials on the battlements, small

The narrow upper gate, Porth Uchaf, now flanked by a path for pedestrians, was originally the only entrance to the walled town on the landward side.

Porth Isaf, the lower gate, the entrance to the town from the harbour, originally led straight onto the shingle of the foreshore.

Porth y Felin, the mill gate, led to the town's mill by the Gyffin stream and is now a main pedestrian access to the town. In the left-hand tower can be seen the post-holes for the ramp up which the materials were wheeled during the town's construction. An interesting feature visible on the wall to the left is a row of twelve privies, jutting out from the wall-walk.

spikes of stone with a purely decorative purpose, intended to lighten the otherwise rather heavy effect of the massive towers, tell us that the builders were concerned that this highly-developed military weapon should please the eye as well as impress the imagination.

The extent of its completeness, and of its state of unaltered preservation, makes Conwy now an example of a medieval walled borough unique in Britain and one of a very small number in the whole of Europe.

The town as first constructed had only three gates. These were strongly defended, with twin towers overlooking their approaches. The Upper Gate, 'Porth Uchaf', the only one on the landward side, was the route by which the people of the countryside would bring their goods to town. The town had its own mill, down by the Gyffin river, and access to this was by the Mill Gate, 'Porth y Felin'. But the main focus of Conwy's communications always was, as it still to a large extent is, the river; and the Lower Gate, 'Porth Isaf', which then gave directly onto the shingle foreshore, was probably the busiest entrance to the town.

The castle was not just a garrisoned fortress; it was constructed as well to be suitable for use as a royal residence. Perhaps partly for that reason it was in two halves, the inner keep being self-contained and further defended against the possible occupation of the outer one — just as the castle as a whole formed a defensive retreat if the town around it fell. Edward himself stayed in the castle at least twice, once in the spring of 1284, on his way to Caernarfon, where his son, the first English Prince of Wales, was born. Ten years later he was here again, and occupied again the rooms in the 'king's tower', but now under less happy circumstances, on his way to try to put down the rebellion of Madoc ap Llywelyn. In an ambush near Bangor he lost his baggage train, and retreated to Conwy's protection short of supplies. During the winter of 1294 and the first weeks of 1295 he looked out from the terrace and the royal apartments over a flooded river, the swollen currents cutting off his supplies from England. The castle fell short of food and wine, and the king suffered along with his men. When the flood abated and help and provisions arrived, we are told they celebrated a late Christmas there in the Great Hall.

Medieval Conwy

FROM time to time throughout later history the castle came into sudden prominence. Its strong walls were attractive to kings in need of security, and for a time it remained in the possession of the crown. In 1399 King Richard II, one of England's more unfortunate kings, was on his way back from Ireland to confront the rebellion of Henry Bolingbroke, Duke of Lancaster, who was by then at Chester. The powerful Earl of Northumberland, acting for Bolingbroke, came to bargain with the king at Conwy. Unknown to Richard he had left a party waiting in ambush, and his mission was to tempt the king out of the castle and along the coast, to meet the rebel baron at Flint. The treacherous Northumberland offered him safe-conduct to Flint and, according to the Chronicle, swore an oath in the chapel of Conwy Castle, to the effect that Richard would be safe.

Convinced by this, Richard rode out from Conwy towards where the Earl's troops were waiting, under Penmaenrhos head, that crag beyond where Colwyn Bay is now, on the north coast. (O.S. SH 878 779.)

> *The Earl rode apace untill hee came where he might see his people under the mountains, whom he much commended for observing his commandment. The king passing the water rode a foure miles before hee came to the rocke; when he saw the ambushes he was sore abashed, knowing well he was betrayed by the Earle, for he was in such as place as he could not escape. The sea beating on the one side and the rocke keeping him on the other, and if he should have fled backe, they would have caught him, ere he could have come to Conway, for hee hadde not past three and twenty of all his company.*

As a result of this betrayal Richard became the prisoner of Bolingbroke, who in due course was to bring about his death, having by then usurped the throne and become King Henry IV. And so the throne of England changed lineages, and Conwy was involved, not for the last time, in a matter of dynasties. Conwy's fortifications were called into use again in the events which

Richard II, crowned at the age of ten in 1377, was lured out of the security of Conwy Castle in 1399 to be taken prisoner and later assassinated by the Duke of Lancaster, Henry Bolingbroke, who usurped his throne and became Henry IV. (Portrait inset).

Aberconwy House, dating from the thirteenth century, is the oldest house in Conwy. Its style is probably characteristic of the houses built by the more prosperous merchants in the Middle Ages.

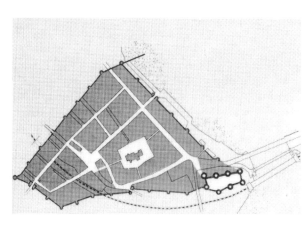

The form of the present town of Conwy is still that of the medieval street pattern, a framework filling the inside of the walls.

followed, the rebellion of Owain Glyndŵr (in which the town was taken and set on fire by the rebels in 1401) and the long turbulence of the Wars of the Roses, in which it several times changed hands.

In the meantime a more substantial medieval town had come into being. When Conwy was not being besieged or attacked it was trading, and no doubt the houses of merchants and shipowners grew more impressive during this time. Though none of these early houses remain, they would have looked similar in style, structure, and size to the one known as Aberconwy House, Conwy's oldest domestic building, which was probably built in the late 13th century, not long after the castle and walls. Its survival of at least two conflagrations may be due to its stone-built base, when other private houses were more probably made entirely of wood, and this in turn implies (as does its size and prominent position) a prosperous owner. Now lovingly restored by the National Trust, it presents, inside, its various phases of use.

What has remained from the time of Conwy's evident rise to prosperity in the Middle Ages until today, is the pattern of the structure of the town which came into being when the area within the walls became more densely filled. The medieval streets were laid out in a simple square pattern parallel to the walls, broken by the focal points of the town's main square and of the central precinct of the Parish Church. This is the pattern on which the Conwy of later ages has been based, and it forms the framework of the town we live in now.

The traditions of the place at the end of the fifteenth century still remained, after two hundred years, those of a garrison town. The English families brought by Edward I to form a colony in Wales had evidently succeeded in establishing themselves, so that they thought of the town still as an English stronghold and resented the occasional infiltration of the Welsh, whom they called foreigners. A long letter of complaint to the king makes this clear. They asked him "for the continual edification in nourishing of Englishmen", to rule that

> *no foreigner shall occupy or use any manner of craft or merchandize, within the said towns and franchises, without licence and agreement of the said burgesses. Also, that from henceforth no man be admitted as burgess of the said towns, but mere Englishmen and of good demeanour . . . Also, that according to the Statute of Rhuddlan, and ordinance of North Wales, Welshmen shall purchase no land within the English town or franchise of the same . . . Also, that the porter of Conwey, which is now a Welshman, may be put out, and the office given to an English Burgess inhabiting in the said town . . . for it is no more meet for a Welshman to bear any office in Wales, or especially in any of the three English towns, than it is for a Frenchman to be officer in Calais, or a Scot in Berwick.*

21

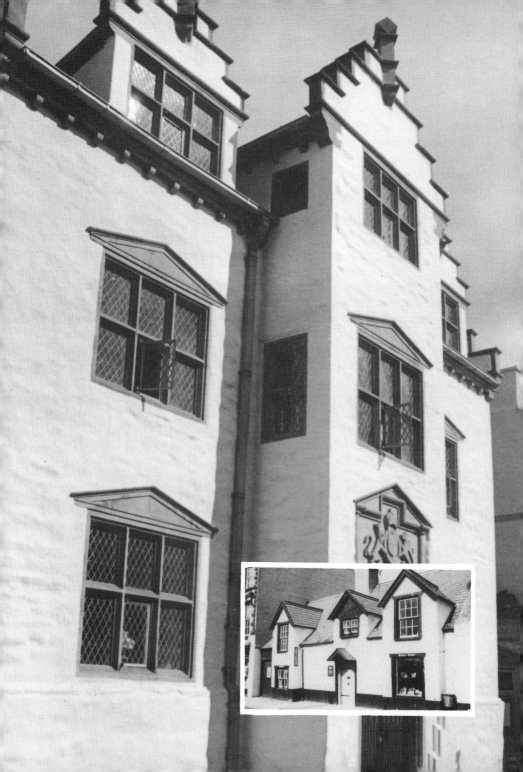

The Renaissance

THINGS were changing; now there was a Welsh king in London and Welshmen were in favour. Just as Conwy has played its part in the long course of British history, in spite of its distance from the centre of events, similarly its own fortunes have changed with the changing state of the rest of the country. Now that the opportunities of advancement were available, the great families of North Wales were not slow to take them up. It is to this period that the rise to power and wealth of such families as those of the Hollands, the Mostyns, and the Wynns (or Wynnes), belongs, which in turn gave us in this area the great Tudor houses which still ornament our countryside.

In the middle of the reign of Queen Elizabeth I, Robert Wynne built himself a magnificent town house in Conwy, Plas Mawr, taking up a block fronting the High Street, in the middle of the town. With its fine stonework and its beautifully decorated ceilings it shows us the tastes of a new age, the elevated style and the grandeur with which the Renaissance had by then replaced the simpler life of the Middle Ages. Now in the ownership of the Welsh Office, it begins a new life after a painstaking process of restoration which was urgently necessary to preserve its fine interior details from decay.

Looking around Conwy we can see the changing style in humbler buildings too, such as the one in Castle Street which became the Black Lion inn in the 18th century, built as a family house by a Vicar of Conwy in the year 1589.

Though Conwy seemed to be rising towards prosperity, and its medieval armaments seemed to be a thing of the past, its time of war was not yet over. Through much of the reign of Elizabeth, England had a war in Ireland on its hands, and troops passed through Conwy or assembled there on their way to fight. But war came nearer home in the next century, when Conwy was embroiled again in national affairs.

One of the town's more memorable characters was born in 1582, in the reign of Elizabeth, in an old medieval house in Chapel Street of which now, unfortunately, we have little more than the memory. By the time Charles I was on the throne this Conwy man, John Williams, had risen to the prominent position of Archbishop of York. Archbishop Williams was a royalist, and when the Civil War between Charles and Parliament broke out he found

Plas Mawr, a fine Elizabethan town house in the High Street, now restored by the Welsh Office, is a good example of the grander architecture which arose with the Renaissance.

(Inset) The 'Black Lion', at one time an inn, was built by a Vicar of Conwy in the reign of Elizabeth I.

Only ruins are left now of 'Parlwr Mawr', the medieval house in Chapel Street which was the family home of Archbishop John Williams.

Archbishop Williams, born in Conwy in 1582, rose to high office in the reign of Charles I. He was Archbishop of York at the time of the Civil War, and as a prominent supporter of the king he fled to the security of Conwy, where he later changed sides and took part in the siege of the town.

himself in isolation at York, in danger from the Parliamentary army moving north. He fled back here to his home town, no doubt remembering its substantial walls; and in doing so he brought Conwy back into history.

The castle had by then fallen into considerable disrepair, and the Archbishop set about restoring it at his own expense. It was not long before these precautions proved necessary, since Parliament's army under General Mytton marched into North Wales in 1646, and in the summer of that year began to attack Conwy. But by then the king's cause seemed to be failing throughout Britain, and in North Wales it was further damaged by the wilful behaviour of the royalist leaders. Archbishop Williams was incensed by the insulting treatment he received from the man whom the king appointed as governor of Conwy, to the extent that he eventually reacted by changing sides. When Mytton attacked the walls of Conwy in the August of 1646 it was with the support of Williams' advice. In fact the sixty-four-year-old man of God took part himself in the attack, to the extent of being slightly wounded.

They scaled the south walls, and the town fell. The army and the archbishop then besieged the garrison in the castle, which amazingly held out until November — a testimony to the castle's strength, even in those days of cannons and muskets. The fabric of the building was much damaged in the process, and finally the royalists surrendered.

It was another step towards the execution of the king, and all the changes which that was to bring about. And this was to be Conwy's last battle, the last use of the fortifications for their original purpose, warfare.

It was from then on that the place became a ruin. The roof timber was growing rotten, and in 1665 its owner took the opportunity to strip it of its lead and iron, and left us with the gaunt bones of a building which we have today. But though the castle's active life was now over, that of the town was really only just beginning.

Road and Railway

CONWY'S role had always been connected with communications. It lies at the crucial position of the joining of land routes with marine ones. When business and travel became increasingly active during the 18th century Conwy came more and more into prominence. On the one hand the port enabled the produce from the hinterland, which now included coal and slate, to be taken up and down the coast. On the other hand the same river which facilitated this proved, as people began to move around the country more and more, an obstacle to their land-bound journeys. For hundreds of years the crossing of the Conwy was by ferry, either up the river at Tal-y-cafn (O.S. SH 786 719), from where a road ran across a mountain pass, or here at the estuary, where there was an inn on the eastern bank to house travellers waiting for the ferry (O.S. SH 789 779), the passage of which was governed by the state of the tide.

The town in the meantime thrived on this increasing trade. Its streets became full of coaching inns and lodging houses, and its people gained the unfortunate reputation of living mainly by exploiting travellers. The ferrymen were grasping and offensive, the river-crossing dangerous and subject to delays, and as the rise in traffic between north-west England and the ports for Ireland grew with the corresponding growth of the cities of Liverpool and Dublin, it became apparent that something would have to be done about the Conwy crossing.

During the last decades of the 18th century complaints and suggestions began to increase. The engineer John Rennie submitted a plan in 1802, which would have crossed by a causeway similar to that eventually adopted, but would then have passed at a high level through the middle of the castle itself. A tragedy on Christmas Day, 1806, when only two out of fifteen passengers on the ferry survived a capsizing in a heavy swell, perhaps brought the pressure of public opinion to bear on the authorities. Parliamentary Commissions began to consider the problem, and Thomas Telford submitted his scheme to one of these in the year 1811.

The committees delayed this decision for another ten years, while Telford himself, by continuing work on the roads between Chester and North Wales, made the problem of the Conwy crossing more imperative. Holyhead was increasingly establishing itself as the natural port for Ireland, and when the decision to build the Menai Bridge was made in 1818 it was clear that the delay at Conwy could not be tolerated for much longer.

Before the building of the bridges the river was crossed by ferry, from a point near to the present flyover at Llandudno Junction.

27

Telford's suspension bridge, built between 1821 and 1826, jutting in the shape of a draw-bridge from below the castle's terrace, shows a respectful deference to the medieval architecture.

To take his new coast road out of the town Telford adapted one of the wall-towers to make a new gateway, the 'Bangor Arch'.

Telford's plan for a causeway and a bridge, linking the little island in the middle of the current to the eastern bank by an earth embankment and to the castle rock by a suspension bridge, was approved in 1821, and started the next year. By the summer of 1826 the whole scheme was completed, at the cost, it seems, of a little more than fifty thousand pounds. The bridge, now in the care of the National Trust, is both an engineering and an architectural masterpiece, relating, with its towers and crenellations, to the medieval style of the castle, its delicate scale at the same time avoiding obtrusion. In a lengthy restoration process later Victorian work has been removed and the bridge is now presented in the form in which Telford built it.

In the process Telford's plan had had several important effects on the town. By his embankment he had set the route for future crossings of the river. By continuing the habit established by the ferry of feeding the traffic directly into the streets of the town he set the pattern of future problems. The main road, it was now clear, was to continue to run through Conwy. And in the process Telford had to carry out some radical alterations to the medieval structure.

The walls were breached, for the first time, in Castle Square, where Telford built a new entrance and a gateway, since removed. They were breached again at the top end where the new Bangor road left the town, where one of the original wall-towers was converted by Telford into the present Bangor Arch. These two new entrances to the town changed the layout and form of what was previously a much more enclosed place. From now on, of course, it was to become busier year by year, and thrown more and more into contact with the outside world.

These were times of great advances in technological achievement. Hard behind the road came the railway, driving its metal tracks along the north coast of Wales during the 1840s. Once again Conwy was honoured by the attentions of one of the great engineers of the time, when Robert Stephenson undertook the task of setting a tubular railway-bridge alongside Telford's suspension bridge, twenty years later, in 1846. This, like Telford's, is a fine piece of architecture in itself, with its massive battlemented towers with their many fine touches of respectful reference to their older neighbour — although in this case, unlike that of Telford's more light-handed work, the structure is so bulky as to compete more than is desirable. The towers were built large enough to take a supporting cable if the span proved too long — unnecessarily, as it turned out, since when, towards the end of the last century, the structure did shift slightly out of line, the solution favoured was the reduction of the span by the use of cylindrical supports at either end. The bridge was built by constructing the towers first, building the tube in sections a little way upriver, then floating the sections down and hoisting them into place.

Stephenson's massive tubular bridge carries the railway across the river to a new embankment at the foot of the castle above the Gyffin stream.

Where the railway passed through the town wall Stephenson reconstructed the wall in the form of a pointed archway.

The characteristic cottages of the late 18th and early 19th centuries in Conwy show the distinctive features of the local vernacular style. The smooth surfaces at the bottom of the walls and around the windows and doorways are picked out in dark colours, contrasting with the lighter shades used for the pebble-dash rendering of the walls.

The highly distinctive facade of a Welsh chapel bulks over the streets of small cottages, in Conwy as in all Welsh towns.

It was one of the effects of Telford's decision to cross the river by embankment that the course of the railways followed so closely that of the road. The railway, like the road, passed right through the town. The rock on which the castle stands was banked outwards, the castle now being bracketed by the two routes. Just as Telford had to alter the physical structure of Conwy walled town to get his road through, so now Stephenson again needed to breach the walls. To be fair to him he did the alterations with the greatest possible care and discretion, flanking the terrace on which the track passed the castle·with suitably grand turrets and rebuilding the wall, where it went through, into an appropriately noble and attractive archway.

Conwy's railway period was another time of activity, with the digging of the great cutting and the continuing of the line-laying onwards to Holyhead no doubt providing employment on a new scale for people in the town.

Conwy, in the meantime, had never stopped its traditional business, that of the harbour and the quay. Just before the end of the 18th century, William Wordsworth, on a visit to North Wales, had put on record this association, that Conwy evidently had by then, with sea-going, in the poem 'We are Seven', which he set in Conwy's churchyard.

> Sisters and brothers, little Maid,
> How many may you be?"
> "How many? Seven in all," she said,
> And wondering looked at me.
>
> "And where are they? I pray you tell."
> She answered, "Seven are we;
> And two of us at Conway dwell,
> And two are gone to sea."

We can infer that the fifty years after Wordsworth's time saw here, as in so many places, a large increase in commercial activity. During the late 18th and early 19th centuries, we can see, there was considerable rebuilding. Conwy was now a busy port, with boats bringing slate down the river to load onto larger sea-going vessels for export all over the world. No doubt it was then, as it always had been, a fishing-port as well as a freight dock. We find much evidence in the graveyard for this emphasis on shipping and the sea. It is largely to this period too that the characteristic cottages belong, in which lived the families of the many people who worked on the ships and in the port.

One thing that is also clear is that by now the Welsh, ironically categorised by the original burgesses as 'foreigners', and excluded by law from the town, had quietly moved in and taken over. By the 19th century, at least, Conwy had become, with its terrace cottages and its imposing chapels, in both style and outlook, a thoroughly Welsh town.

In many ways our present century has not been a lovely or a lovable one. Sometimes we cannot help feeling that circumstances have developed rather faster than our ability to control them. Throughout this story we have seen the effects on Conwy of the relentlessly increasing activity of the progressing world, an increase mainly in movement, in sheer coming and going.

Since its early days Conwy has been to a greater or lesser extent connected with transport, and has both benefitted and suffered from this connection. This century has seen the town bedevilled by traffic problems and resultant road plans as never before. One of the less fortunate results of this is the road bridge built in the 1950s, which alienates the castle from its natural relationship with the river. This new crossing also perpetuated the traffic problem from which the town was by then suffering, the mistake — as it had by then turned out to be — of directing the main road traffic into the town streets; and almost as soon as it was built it was clear that the problem still remained to be solved. The solution — the first immersed tube tunnel to be built in Britain — was completed in 1991, and set Conwy on a new phase of its long and complex history. Now by-passed, it has regained some of the self-respect which its years of traffic-jam had drained from it. Its physical fabric has been the subject of much attention, with (for instance) a new layout for the main square.

In the meantime Conwy goes about its business. The life of the town goes on. Conwy's past is the story of how it received the influence of outside forces, adapting both them and itself to produce a new result. Those who know the town would agree that it has been successful, in the process, in resisting the erosion of its character which might have taken place, so that it still remains today, after so many changes, distinctly and unapologetically Conwy. Conwy's present is not that of a preserved specimen of history; it has survived not only as an interesting example of medieval architecture but as a town. Not as a relic, but as a living survival. Its character and attractiveness and the affection which it commands have not come about by themselves, but rather as a result of a long and sometimes painful process. What you see around you is the form which the past takes in the present.